Meth, God, and My Heart
A True Story of Recovery

Austin Brothers
— PUBLISHING —
www.abpbooks.com

Meth, God, and My Heart
A True Story of Recovery

Foster Chambers

"A man's story of meth addiction, his belief in God, and how both affected his heart."

Meth, God, and My Heart
A True Story of Recovery

Foster Chambers

Published by Austin Brothers Publishing, Fort Worth, Texas
www.abpbooks.com

Copyright 2022 by Foster Chambers

The copyright supports and encourages the right to free expression. The purpose is to encourage writers and artists to continue producing work that enriches our culture.

Scanning, uploading, and distribution of this book without permission by the publisher is theft of the author's intellectual property. To obtain permission to use material from the book (other than for review purposes) contact terry@abpbooks.com.

ISBN: 978-1-7375807-9-9

Printed in the United States of America
2022 -- First Edition

This book and the powerful story it tells,
is dedicated to
"My Beautiful Firstborn"
My Wife and My Parents

Contents

Introduction	11
How It Started, You Ask?	15
Some Improvements but New Problems	23
One of the Worst Decisions of My Life	31
A Devastating Loss	41
Looking for a Replacement	49
Putting Life Back Together	57
A Broken Heart – Physically and Emotionally	63
Thoughts on Addiction	69
Epilogue	77

*On the following pages,
you will discover a painful
but true story of a man's struggle
against overwhelming odds.
This is not a feel-good story with
a happy ending, but it is a
story that will affect you deeply.*

INTRODUCTION

THERE WAS a history of sexual abuse by my mother's boyfriend, Doug. However, after they married, he came to me and promised it would no longer happen now that he was my father. It was hard to believe it would just stop, but things were better for several weeks. I was only eleven years old, so there wasn't much I could do.

When I came home one evening, the sound of "Maggie" by Rod Stewart was blaring on the radio. I went to my room to change clothes. After a few minutes, I heard screaming and banging over the loud music. Without waiting to get dressed, I ran to the kitchen to see what was happening. That's when my nightmares once again became my reality. I don't know precisely what happened, but Doug had physically beaten Mom. Somehow, she escaped and ran to the neighbor's house to call the police. When Doug saw me, he grabbed me and threw me to the floor.

In a matter of seconds, he was sitting on top of me, holding me down with one hand and waving a bayonet with the other. He was screaming and cursing, blaming me for something, but I had no idea what he was talking about. Hearing the clamor from the house as they arrived, the police crashed through the front door. When Doug looked up at them, he screamed, "I'll kill him, I swear I will!"

The standoff was like you see in the movies, with the hostage-taker threatening to kill the hostage and the police maneuvering to get in the right position. It probably all happened in less than a minute, but as a kid, I knew I was about to die. At one point, Doug turned the wrong way to reposition himself. One of the police officers seized the opportunity and was able to disarm him and set me free. My body was flush with adrenaline.

It was February in Illinois, the sun was down, and it was freezing cold. That didn't stop me. I shot out the front door, running down the street. My underwear was the only clothing to protect me from the cold. I'm not quite sure why I was running, but I was going as fast as I could.

I didn't get too far before a police officer caught me. He wrapped me up and carefully put me in his car. He said, "I'm sorry, little man. I know you've been put through the wringer."

I said, "Please make sure you tell him I didn't tell."

The officer was curious and asked what I meant, but I didn't respond. I was afraid to tell anyone about the way I was treated. After everyone was settled, Mom packed up everything, and we moved away once again. Our typical pattern when things blew up.

At this point, I would love to throw in an "I lived happily ever after" comment, but it's not true. Getting out of the house and moving away from Doug didn't solve any problems. He was neither the beginning of my struggles nor the end. In order to tell my complete story, we need to go back to when I was five years old. As the title suggests, it's a story of *Meth, God, And My Heart*.

My last shot of meth was late in the afternoon of May 19, 2020. I stuck the needle into the top of my hand, between my middle and ring fingers. I missed the sweet spot. Injecting the wrong spot is one of the worst things to happen to an IV drug user, especially with meth. It burns, creates a large swollen area, and there is no high from the drug.

Even though my last injection was more than two years ago, I still struggle with my addiction as I write this book. It has been a forty-five year struggle out of fifty years of my life. Addiction is experienced by many people. My addiction is to drugs, specifically meth. For others, it might be lust or pornography, or even vanity, overeating, or a myriad of other issues. Some addictions are more destructive than others, but they all create havoc in our lives. But I'm still here.

The reason I'm still here is that in addition to all the terrible things you will read in my story, you will also hear about some good things. Most notably among them is God. To be honest, I don't understand why I went through such a difficult struggle or why I did the things I did. As you read my story, I know what will go through your mind— "How can this guy call himself a Christian? How can he write a book about God?"

I find some solace in words found in the Bible. "I do not understand what I do. For what I want to do I do not do, but what I hate I do." (Romans 7:15). That scripture says it all. I hate doing what I do, but I continue doing it, knowing it's wrong but unable to stop. You might be tempted to say that's just an excuse for doing wrong, but you would be mistaken. It's a day-to-day life struggle, one that I've dealt with since I was a young boy.

Everyone who picks up this book wrestles with sin. It might not be an addiction, but we all sin. Sin is sin! God doesn't count any person's sin greater than another's. It is humans who rate some sins as worse than others, not God. What He sees is that sin separates us from God. Even something you might consider the slightest sin separates you from God. Don't judge me that my sin is worse than yours. I'm not trying to get you to approve of my sin; I never will. All I want is for you to see me how God sees all of us.

My hope is that you will join me on this journey. My prayer is that you will discover God's help as I did. If someone with the life experiences I've had can find help and hope, you can too. Keep reading, and you just yet might find victory.

Foster's Journal

It's 2 a.m. here in Chicago. The devil woke me up a bit early this morning. I've struggled with nightmares all my life. I only remember a week that I went without them, and that ended up a nightmare in itself. I had dinner with Mom's best friend last night. I've known her ever since I was a little boy. I love her, but like the rest of the people that know our family dynamics, the past always becomes part of the conversation.

I never let anyone speak against my mom. I don't care what she did; let happen, did or didn't do. She's my mom. I always defend her honor.

Norma did not speak negatively about my mom. However, she is always honest. I give her a bit more leeway than others too.

I still carry the heaviness of my childhood. I still feel shame that isn't mine to feel, but I feel it the same. I still have violent, intense nightmares of being tortured. Even though they can no longer hurt me physically, they continue to abuse me emotionally in the middle of the night during sleep. I have no negative feelings towards my mom or the men who hurt me. At least, I don't think so?

I don't care about all this stuff that's happened to me. It made me who I am, and by the grace of God, I could use it to help others. I just don't want it to affect my sleep anymore. It's exhausting.

How It Started, You Ask?

MOST FIVE-YEAR-OLDS are playing in the yard with their friends, learning the letters of the alphabet, preparing to read, perhaps getting on a bike with training wheels, and excited about starting school soon. When I was five years old, I smoked my first cigar, and it went downhill from there. On that same day, my fifth birthday, I also smoked my first joint and drank my first beer. It was a day of firsts.

My older brother and uncle had me smoke marijuana. It seems I was a funny sight, trying to ride my bike while high. It was like I was their science project. They filled me with drugs and liquor and then added the admonition, "Don't tell Mom."

Mom was on her third marriage by this time, and our lives had never been easy. Life involved a great deal of physical and emotional abuse. It's not an overstatement to say it was torture. I was physically struck every day. I constantly heard that Mom's husband hated me.

It's not a surprise that I was a chronic bed wetter. More than once a night, sometimes twice. It was not purposeful; it just happened. I also suffered from night terrors and occasional sleepwalking. I would wake up in different parts of the house screaming in terror, and Mom would come to get me. In kindergarten and first grade, Steve made me wear diapers to school just to humiliate me.

Steve was a mean man. I remember him as a big man, huge for a little guy like me. He was probably well over six feet tall. The night terrors started the minute he and Mom got married. They both worked at the same factory, and there was a time when she was put on the night shift, which meant I was home all night with Steve and his sister Tina.

After every bed wetting incident, Steve tortured me. I specifically remember one incident. After wetting the bed, Steve took me to the laundry room in the basement. He placed the urine-soaked sheets on my head and commanded, "Bend over."

I knew what was coming and refused. That was followed by dancing around the room, trying to deflect the blows of his belt. He said, "Fine! You don't want a beating. You can stay here until you're ready to!"

He made me stand in the laundry room with the soiled sheet on top of my head. I was not allowed to sit, use the restroom (which caused me to urinate again), eat, drink, or speak to anyone. I remained in that position overnight into the next day.

My half-sister and brother, who lived in another town, were visiting us at the time. They lived with their father. When Steve went upstairs, my half-sister snuck in a few pieces of food and some water in the middle of the night. She also made sure I wasn't sitting down or sleeping. On the second day, I gave in. I told Steve, "You can beat me; I deserve it."

He laughed and said, "You're a piece of shit! Get outta my sight."

We also had a dog, an Irish Setter named Kelly, that Steve taught to chase me around the yard. I wasn't allowed to step into the living room or speak at the table. If I put an elbow on the

Meth, God, and My Heart

table, my arm would be slammed down on the table so hard that I thought it might break.

I've always been soft-spoken, and I would describe myself as gentle as a kid. I loved Evil Knievel and Superman. My biggest hero was The Fonz from the TV show Happy Days. I had a leather jacket and loved wearing a Fonzie t-shirt. I rode my Big Wheel everywhere I went. I always loved being around girls, even though the other boys tormented them. I catered to them, walked them home, and cared about them. My love for women became kind of a love/hate thing as I aged.

I have no idea why Steve hated me so much, but he definitely did. His sister, Tina, on the other hand, loved me very much. It was also around that same time that I had my first encounter with the female body. Tina would call me into her bedroom, where she would fondle me and then make me perform sexual acts on her. I was so young that I didn't realize it was wrong. One day, Steve came into the room and caught us on the bed together. I thought I was in for another beating. Instead, he said, "Don't stop," as he stood in the corner and touched himself.

Even as a five-year-old, it didn't feel right; kind of dirty and disgusting. That evening, I remember Mom asked me several times what was wrong. I said, "Steve's mad at me."

She assured me, "No, honey, he loves you. He's not mad at you."

As far as I know, my mom was not aware of what happened that day.

As I aged, I realized my parents were completely in touch with their sexuality. Perhaps it would be more accurate to say obsessed. Frequently, I woke up in the middle of the night, only to find Mom in bed with another man or multiple men, none of whom was my stepdad. I discovered they were "swingers" and entertained key parties with other couples.

The first time I saw my mother nude was an accident. I walked into the bathroom, not knowing she was in the bathtub. She spanked me repeatedly for my mistake. For someone who put herself out there with multiple men, she sure got extremely angry with me for seeing her nude.

Mom and Steve's house was huge. I remember it felt like a castle. Our family was well-known in the community. Many people were in and out of our house. Mom and Steve's bedroom was enormous and took up most of the second floor. Their bed was up on a platform, and five steps were required to reach the mattress. It was located in the center of the room, surrounded by mirrors and lights. It was crazy, especially on Saturday nights when there was always a party.

Saturday nights included people from our community and others from out of town. I would wake up in the middle of the night and find Mom doing three different guys, and in another room, Steve was always with somebody else. Drugs were rampant. I remember we had a pinball machine, and there was cocaine all over it. I didn't know what it was at the time. It was a confusing life.

Friday nights were different. Most nights, I was not allowed into the living room for fear that I would break something. I was required to sit in the hallway on the edge of the carpet to watch television or be involved in anything else going on. However, on Friday nights, around Johnny Carson time, I sat with my parents in front of the TV. Mom always gave me a cup of apricot juice. The next thing I knew was waking up in bed. After falling asleep, Mom would carry me upstairs.

One of my fingers was always pricked, and there was a band-aid. I found out later that Steve was doing Satanic rituals with me in the basement. I remember the room having black carpet, red walls, and a big pentagram in the center. The room scared the crap out of me. I don't know what they were doing because I was always asleep. He was doing Satanic rituals as some kind of means of gaining money, and I'm sure there was abuse going on at the same time.

This went on for several years. He beat me all the time, his sister also. I can remember at six and seven years of age, making marijuana pipes. I figured out that it would help me by taking away some of the pain. This abuse was daily life for me. I accepted it as normal life until I was eventually allowed to spend the night at a friend's house. I saw how his dad actually played with us, and we were allowed to sit in the living room. This was all new to me, especially when his dad hugged and said, "I love you guys." All that time, I thought my life was normal.

I survived my childhood by the grace of God. My teachers saw me covered with bruises but said nothing. It was back in the 70s, a different time. Nobody talked about family abuse. What happened in your home, stayed in the home. It was much different than today. In First Grade, I had to get glasses, and they gave me big horned-rimmed pair. The doctor went to adjust them, and Steve said no, so I wore them that way. I have a first-grade photo of me wearing those crooked big horned-rimmed glasses.

The day came when Steve beat Mom so bad she had to have her jaw wired. Her face was black and blue, covered with bruises. That was enough for Mom, and she threw him out. Two weeks later, Doug was there, living with us.

Doug wasn't physically abusive to me like Steve; his abuse was sexual. When he began dating Mom, she was working the second shift. The first time of abuse occurred when I was in the bathroom, sitting on the toilet. Doug entered the room and stood in front of me. He pulled his penis out of his pants and told me to suck it. I looked at him like he was crazy. He reached out, grabbed the back of my head, and shoved my face into his crotch. It became a regular thing after that.

This went on for about three years until Mom booted Doug out. That was her pattern. She would keep a man until she got hurt, and then it was over.

Coming home from school one afternoon, I found Mom and Doug in the kitchen. She was holding a big pkate of spaghetti. She was naked, and they were laughing about something. Although I was only ten, I said, "What the fuck? Why are you so happy?"

Their news was that they got married earlier in the day. I ran to my room and slammed the door. A few minutes later, Doug came in and said, "I'm your dad now, and what happened before is not going to happen again. I'm sorry."

"Ok," I said. There was a small part of me that wanted to believe it.

Two days later, it was back.

He had promised Mom he would stop drinking, but I came home one night when she was at work, and he was drunk. I didn't say anything to him or Mom. Sometime later, I came home from church on a Wednesday night to see that mom was badly beaten. That's when he came after me with the bayonet from the Salvation Army store. That's why I insisted the cops know that I didn't tell anyone; it wasn't my fault.

After everything was over, we left the house and went to my Grandma's house, where we stayed for a couple of days. After that, we moved into a low-income apartment. I was hoping things would change. They did, but not everything changed for something better.

Foster's Journal

The mind of an addict is...
Dark, Lonely, selfish, manipulating, greedy, perverted, and sad.

It feels pleasure only when it's given what it wants. It focuses on that deed and will do it if they can get it.

It will lie, cause pain, steal, and even be killed, so it doesn't have to ignore the pain and suffering it feels while sober.

The mind of an addict hears whispers from the devil and his demons.

It hears, "you're worthless, you're a failure, you're a liar, a bad person, and you're not worthy of being loved."

The mind of an addict never needs someone to tell them how bad they are; they know every time they look into the mirror.

The mind of an addict wants to be accepted, understood, cared for, and loved. The mind of an addict wants to know someone sees them, hears them, and will help them out of the madness within their mind.

SOME IMPROVEMENTS BUT NEW PROBLEMS

ABOUT A week after moving into the apartment, I answered a knock at the door. That's when I met Ernie. He asked if Sandy was there. I said, "No!" and slammed the door in his face. Obviously, he came back later, and soon they were sleeping together.

When I caught them, I screamed and threw a fit. I asked Mom what I was supposed to do. "I want you to just not need a man," I said. "Why can't it just be us once and not another man?"

They dated for a year and a half before getting married. I was twelve years old. As a kid, being sexually molested ended for a time when Ernie came into our lives. He worked at the same factory as my mom, but he was a drug and alcohol counselor.

My brother was instrumental in getting me hooked on drugs. I was their guinea pig. They handed me stuff to try, not always sure how it would affect me. By age 10 or 11, I was doing more drugs than most adults. By 12, I had a strong cocaine habit. It sounds unbelievable, like someone on the Jerry Springer Show, but it was true. I also recall sneaking into the liquor cabinet and getting drunk. Mom would send me to the store for cigarettes. In those days, a kid could purchase tobacco if they had a note from a parent. One time I was drunk when I left home and passed out while walking down the railroad tracks. After sleeping it off, I walked home, where I was beaten, not for getting drunk but forgetting the cigarettes.

Before Mom and Ernie's wedding, I was sneaking out of the house frequently. I was stealing drugs from my brother's stash, selling them to have money. In a short time, I became the guy in junior high you could go to for dope because I was always available. I provided speed, called White Crosses and Christmas Trees. I also had marijuana. My brother had a temper and kept his stash in a hole in the wall he punched one night. My brother was mad that I was stealing his stuff, but I didn't quit. Drugs were always around, so I didn't think much about them. It was just what I did, and it was a good way to have some money.

When I was 12 years old, I went to church camp. Although it was unlike anything I was accustomed to, it was probably like every other Christian youth camp. We spent the daytime playing games, evenings in a church setting, and nights tormenting roommates and camp leaders. Friday night was the big night of the week, especially for the church service. The other nights were great, but Friday was heavily promoted and highly anticipated.

Throughout the week, we searched for the girl we wanted to date. Remember, I was only 12, so there wasn't much real dating happening. The hope was for some hand-holding at the Friday night service.

The time began like all the previous evenings throughout the week. Prior to worship, they held Bible verse competitions. After a time of worship, the speaker shared. I can't tell you one word he said in the entire message; I was still wrapped up in worship. I wasn't singing out loud but inside, within my soul. I will be still in the presence of my Father. It was that way through the speaker's entire message.

When he announced an altar call, I ran forward. As I sat on the steps at the front of the sanctuary, God gave me a vision. I saw myself standing on a stage as an adult, speaking to hundreds of people. I wasn't dressed in fancy clothes, but I heard myself saying, "If God could take a man like me out of the world, He can surely take you as well." I've had several other visions over the years, but I will never forget that first encounter.

Upon arriving home, I immediately shared my experience with my mom. She said, "That's nice," and acted as if I was just making an off-the-cuff remark. Her comment put doubt in my heart, but it never made me want to let go of that vision.

Ernie, my mom's latest and last husband, was great. We lived in the city, and he had a home in a small community of only twelve hundred people. We moved out to his place. He was a stern man, which I often experienced because I was running wild. I did whatever I wanted until he came around and put a firm grasp on me. He was firm but good for me. He was hard, but I needed it.

Ernie and I had a difficult time seeing eye-to-eye on my life. I wanted to run and do my own thing. He saw my problem and wanted to help. When I was 14, I entered drug treatment for the first time. It happened because I got drunk at a school party and passed out in a rose bush. It was the middle of winter, and the police were called. They took me to rehab. Ernie did everything he could to help me as a teenager, but I was eventually kicked out of high school for selling drugs. Not only was I selling, but I was also using. It was the only way I could cope. Frequent night terrors were so severe that my mom found me outside the house at times., Without drugs, I couldn't make it.

During that first rehab stay, I met my biological father. He came to the rehab center with his much younger wife. They had two kids together. He wasn't looking for me specifically, but my younger brother sought him out, and that led to him wanting to come to see me. That was when I met him and my two little sisters.

Mom's rule was that I either go to school or get a job. Since I was no longer welcome at school, my job became selling drugs. The whole thing was insane because I was considered an outpatient from rehab. During that time, I ended up in a fight with three guys in our front yard. Ernie was angry because I was fighting and didn't turn the other cheek like Jesus said. I don't know how he expected me to do that, so he and I got into it.

When I woke up the next morning, my bags were packed. The entire family got in the car, and they took me to my biological father's house, four hours away. It was a strange feeling as I stood in his living room and listened to Mom explain that I was now his responsibility. She gave me a hug, and they drove off. Fifteen years old and starting over in a new place with people who were essentially strangers.

Even though he was my real father, when my mom and stepdad left, I felt alone. We sat down at a picnic table in the backyard to talk. He asked, "Dude, do you do drugs?"

I just got out of drug rehab, and he asks if I do drugs. "Well yeah, I do drugs."

He gave me a line of coke and a Bud Light.

"While you're here, you're going to school. And you're going to find a job," he explained.

"Well, I'm not going to school. I'll find a job."

Within a short time, I had a job cooking peanuts and cashews at a place called the Nutty Nut Shop. Whenever I got paid, he gave me $20 and took to rest of the check. All we did was party together. When he got really plastered, he would stand over me while he thought I was asleep and say terrible things about my mom. I took it for a short time, but I finally got to where I couldn't handle it anymore. All I knew to do was leave.

Foster's Journal

This is a simple spiritual, not religious, program known as Narcotics Anonymous. We do recover.

I woke up from a dream in tears this morning, which, unfortunately, is odd. What's odd is; that they were tears of joy.

In the dream, I was standing in a circle of people who were praying and worshipping God. Yes, I said the word, god. I seemed to be the only one moving around as if I was high. I was trying to hide it, but it was obvious to myself and others. There was a black man with dreadlocks on my left, and a white woman who I believe was his wife on my right. She said that she was a cardiac nurse.

I told you that my heart was bad. He reached around and laid his hand on the spot where my pacemaker used to be; she put her hand on my right shoulder, and they prayed for me. The power of God came over me, and I started crying, knowing I was healed.

Why do I say that? What does it have to do with recovery?

I think God that NA is not a religious program. God is not religious. Religion is a manmade human viewpoint based on man's ideas of who God is. I do believe in the Bible, but I believe there are things added and things left out for the benefit of man.

I don't go to church, but that's just me. I think church is up to an individual, based on that person's needs.

How many times do people sit in a crowd, acting as if everything is all right, only wanting help, yet ashamed or afraid to ask for it? I know I have.

We want everything to appear perfect. We want our lives to seem put together. I know there ain't no word and June Cleaver in my house. How many times in our churches do we do the same thing? How many addicts are in all these religious places yet are being held captive to their addiction because they don't have anyone to go to or because of fear of being rejected by them? The church can't fix an addict. The spirit of God can.

The spiritual part of recovery is God. The higher power based on a god of my own understanding is leading you to God.

God makes people's stomachs turn. It gets people to agree and makes people quit reading and stroll on by. It makes people lash out.

God takes the heat for the word religion created by man for man's benefit of man's needs. Man hates God because man hates religion. When in fact, God is a simple spiritual, not religious, God who wants you to come to know Him within your own understanding, having a relationship with you.

The creators of AA and NA knew what they were doing when they wrote these programs.

> They let God guide their spirits, and it's helped millions of addicts across the world.

ONE OF THE WORST DECISIONS OF MY LIFE

LEAVING MY father's house meant I had nowhere to go. I had already been thrown out of my mother's place, so that wasn't an option. Although I couldn't stay at her house, the city was the only place I knew. I hopped on a bus and went back to where I came from. For a year, I lived on the streets. I slept in abandoned buildings and scrounged food from garbage cans with a buddy named Bob.

My little brother found me and wanted to help. He explained how he located Ashley, who was my real father's ex-wife. They were recently divorced. She invited me to come there and stay with her. So we did. Bob and I walked 217 miles to have a place to stay, a place to live. Bob lasted a month until we kicked him out.

One night, I woke up in the early hours, and Ashley was on top of me. Despite all of the sexual abuse I had endured, it was the first time I had ever had intercourse with a woman. She got pregnant and was only 21 years old. I was 16 years old at the time, and Ashley was twenty-one. Even though she had been married to my birth father, she was much younger than him. Her being pregnant was made even worse when my mother and stepfather heard about it; they insisted we get married. They were both Christians and serving as ministers and felt like it was the only right thing to do.

Just so you don't get lost in the details, let me reset my situation. I was 16 years old, married to a pregnant wife, and I haven't mentioned that she had two girls by my birth father, so they were actually my half-sisters. However, Ashley insisted they call me Daddy. She told them, "This is your daddy," so they became my children. It sounds like a good country song. They were teenagers before being told by my mom that they were not my daughters. I hated Ashley from the moment we were together. She was psycho.

We were living in Danville, Illinois, the city where I was born. We were dependent on public assistance since I didn't have a job. All I did was drugs and drink. We fought like cats and dogs. Although I never struck Ashley, she beat the hell out of me constantly. Yet, we were together for 23 years.

I was never physically attracted to Ashley. When I lived with my father, she showed me a lot of attention, probably because I was closer to her age than her husband (my father). When she took the girls to the park or somewhere else, she took me along. While Dad was sitting around high on something, she bought cigarettes for me as well as frequent small gifts. As I look back, I think she was setting me up for something else.

We fought every day, often throwing things at each other, and she constantly hit me with her fists. I wasn't allowed to hang out with friends or do anything without her. I lived in extreme shame because of my choice to stay with her. Not only did we struggle to survive financially, but I was also barely hanging on mentally. Although I eventually got my GED and enrolled in some college classes, I quit school and began to seek ways to get away from her.

On uary 21, the day our daughter was born, I was in the room when she entered this world. Immediately, I fell in love for the first time in my life. She was perfect. She was long and thin with beautiful black eyes and a head of black hair. She looked like a little bird. I held her in my arms the first time and said, "I will love and protect you forever." I knew I could never leave this beautiful person God entrusted to me, so I stayed.

Ashley's mom and stepdad lived in Florida, so we packed up and moved south. It was exciting to move, looking for something new. However, I wished I was going with someone else. Orlando was a beautiful place. Her parent's house was not. They were both alcoholics, and by that, I mean drunks. Her mom was a gin drinker, and her stepdad favored beer. They drank from the minute they woke up until they passed out at night. I've seen her mom mess herself in the middle of the night and still be laying in fecal material when she woke the next morning. I even saw her stepdad so intoxicated that he opened a kitchen cabinet and urinated on the pots and pans. They were some of the worst people I have ever met.

They lived in a small, filthy trailer house. He worked as an exterminator, which is ironic since they had the worst infestation of cockroaches I've ever seen. The first shower I took, when I pulled back the shower curtain, I discovered a gigantic turtle surrounded by raw chicken. I couldn't believe how incredibly dirty they were.

He got me a job at the exterminating company where he worked, and once I received a couple of paychecks, we moved to our own place. It was just down the road from Ashley's parents, but it was very nice and clean. Although it was a different place, our lives didn't change. We continued to fight daily, and I hated her more than ever.

My little brother called to ask if he could come and live with us. Without hesitation, I said yes, and he came. We made a nice place for his stay in the attached garage. His presence eased come of the altercations between Ashley and me. In a short time, my brother and I went to work for a company that installed irrigation systems for large condominiums being built along the coastline.

On a typical week, we would leave on Sunday afternoon for the job site and return on Friday afternoon. They paid us well, gave us a condo to stay in, and provided money for food expenses. We loved it. It was easy work that allowed us to hit all the social nightlife and do whatever we wanted without anyone knowing. Most of all, I wasn't with Ashley.

After a while, my brother met a girl, and she got pregnant and had a baby. They eventually moved out, and I was stuck with the person I hated the most. My brother and I were always close and remained that way until the end.

Ashley and I got homesick and decided to move closer to home. A friend of ours was living in a small town in Missouri. Her husband worked for a company as a truck driver that delivered grocery items to convenience stores. He told me the company was hiring drivers and would train me if I got my Class A license. Ashley got a job working as a nursing assistant in one of the local nursing homes. So we ended up in the middle of nowhere in Missouri.

My delivery route was in the area around Branson, Missouri. It was a beautiful scenic route that I loved. However, in the winter it was dangerous because of the snow and ice, but always the views were amazing.

Ashley got pregnant with her second child, a boy. When they placed him on her stomach, I said, "When he's 18, I'm leaving you."

She chuckled, saying, "No, you're silly. You need me, and I'll work it all out."

That night I got drunker than I've ever been. I was extremely excited about having a son. He became my little buddy. I vowed to protect him always, just as I did my daughter the day she was born. Now there were four of us.

Ashley took a job at one of the area turkey processing plants. She worked the night shift, and I worked days driving a truck. One day, she mentioned the plant was hiring drivers and said I should apply. It was less hours, more money, and I would be on the same shift she was on. I figured two out of three wasn't bad.

My job was to drive the turkeys into the plant, where they were removed from the cages and hung on the production line for slaughter. It was the most boring job I've ever had. All I did was ease the truck forward until the trailer was empty. It was washed out, and I picked up another trailer of turkeys. Three drivers worked each shift, and there were a lot of downtimes. Most of the other drivers slept while waiting to get unloaded. Not me. I studied the entire process, from entering the building all the way through processing. I didn't need sleep because I was doing a gram of methamphetamine each night.

The kill floor supervisor was terminated, and the position became available. Since it was a union company, we were allowed to bid for the job. I submitted my name thinking it was better than sitting in a truck doing nothing. I had carefully watched the process for two years.

Only two of us signed up for the job, but I was never interviewed. One night I went to work, and the other man was working the new job we had both applied for. I asked the Superintendent, who told me the other man had more experience, so he gave him the position. Even though I was angry, I accepted the fate until I saw the Plant Manager one day. He was a large man with a reputation for kicking doors off the hinges when he wasn't happy. He was hot-tempered and feared by everyone. He had made the plant one of the most profitable in the entire company.

I walked up to him and said, "I understand the other guy has more experience, but I would have liked to at least be interviewed."

He had a puzzled look, "I didn't even know you signed the bid. The Superintendent told me there was only one person."

When I assured him that I had signed the bid and was very interested in the position, he immediately contacted Human Resources and insisted they set up interviews for the other person and me. During my interview with the Plant Manager, I laid it all out. I spoke of all the issues I had noticed for the past two years, including managing employee relations, productivity, and downtime. He seemed shocked and impressed that I could be a truck driver and still have so much insight into plant issues. The next day I was offered the job of Kill Floor Supervisor. It paid a whopping

$27,000 per year. I worked an extreme number of hours with enormous stress, and I loved it.

During my five years at that plant, I received two promotions, implemented numerous cost-effective programs, and killed the most turkeys in an eight-hour shift in company history—22,485 turkeys in one night. An impressive night, as far as turkey killing goes. Ashley moved up as well and was a supervisor. However, she was disliked by upper management, which she discovered rather quickly when she got upset. She wrote a resignation letter as a threat, but they saw it as an opportunity to let her go.

Ashley and I fought continuously, all day, every day. I didn't know why she wanted to be with me, but I fully understood why I didn't want to be with her. Nothing about our lives was happy. I spent as much time as possible away from home. Now that she wasn't at the plant with me, tensions escalated. I was accused of having affairs and lying about shift times. Even though the accusations were true, I always denied them.

Finally, all her torment made me start looking for another job. We both got on the Internet and secured a recruiter to find us positions within our industry. It didn't take long, and we were on our way south to Mississippi.

We both accepted positions at a poultry plant. I was over the kill floor, and she was over further processing. She worked the second shift, and I worked days. We lived an hour and a half away from the plant, so my days started at 3 am. It was miserable.

My parents came to visit, and my dad asked if I would be interested in working as a drug counselor in the prison at home. He was unaware that I was still in active addiction and could be considered an alcoholic. He said that I could get my addictions license and stay with them until I found a house.

The only problem was that they didn't have room for all of us. The truth was that he despised Ashley and didn't want her in his home. Ashley went to Florida to her parents with three of the children, while I took my "beautiful firstborn" daughter with me.

I tested for my licensure and passed my license on the first try. I was an employee of the Department of Corrections, working in the drug unit. I had a caseload of thirty prisoners, ranging from theft to murder. I enjoyed the position, and the inmates responded to me well. I guess they should have. I was just as much a criminal as all of them.

I worked alongside two women counselors who had been there for a long time. One of them was nice and genuinely cared for the inmates. The other one slept with inmates, caused issues on the unit, and considered me a threat. I had started a new program I had developed, and she wanted nothing to do with it.

I received a call from an investigator within the prison, asking me to come in early. When I got to work, they immediately sent me to the Warden's office, where numerous people were sitting. The Warden said, "You have been accused of inmate aggravation, sexual harassment, and not following the prison's drug program."

I was shocked, but I answered their questions honestly and without hesitation. I was then sent to the Investigation office, where I was briefed. I was placed on suspension following an investigation.

A week later, I was back in the Warden's office with his decision. He said, "Upon investigation, we find you without fault for any of the accusations and believe the accusations were given to remove you from your position."

I sighed with relief, believing I had just won this issue. He then said, "I still have to terminate you. I have two female union employees claiming all of these things. If I don't terminate you, the prison will be facing a lawsuit."

Being in a management role for the last seven years, I completely understood his thought process, ending my career in the Department of Corrections.

We moved all the time. Back and forth from down south, to my hometown, back to the town we met in. Ashley would get mad at me and hit me. The kids would run into their rooms, and she'd keep hitting me. The thing is, she would violently scream as if I was hitting her. She always played the victim. It took 25 years later for her to admit to my children that I didn't beat her. All of their childhood, they thought I was a wife-beater. We continued down this path for many years, 23, to be exact. I was completely hooked on meth and alcohol.

Foster's Journal

I just responded to a post about hearing voices after using a certain drug.

This made me extremely hated, but you're completely correct about it being demonic. However, it is not just meth. It's every addiction. Doctors, scientists, and mental health professionals call addiction a disease because they are not able to solve the issue. They labeled it a disease because it goes against every bit of schooling they've ever been taught. Plus, the demonic spiritual force goes against every bit of scientific evidence they could prove. Addiction is not a disease; it's a demon that orbits the addicted. It's a demon that comes back seven times stronger after a relapse. It's a demon that is cunning and baffling.

That's why it knows what you're trying to do when you're trying to get clean. You go this way; so does your mind. You go that way; so does your mind. Is that the disease of addiction that tried to kill you? It's the Demonic forces that the devil has used to try and kill you since you found out you liked a substance, thing, or act that made you push down all your heartache, trauma, and pain. It's why you hear things telling you things like you're terrible, unloved, useless, and can't be fixed. In my opinion, every time we say, "Hi, I'm such and such, and I'm an addict," it gives the devil something to hold onto. We don't have to be addicts. We don't have to say we're addicted. There is deliverance and freedom that can be had. God can completely deliver a person from ever wanting a drug again. I know, I said God and people hate that word. He's real. He wants us free from the bondage of drugs. We just have to believe it and receive it.

Goes against everything rehab teaches us and the book. You'd never have to call yourself an addict again, and you never have to use again.

The voices you're hearing are demotic. Pray and fight them with the word of God. They must leave. Then fill that void with worship, prayer, and reading the word of God. You'll notice they will go away.

Let the slams against what I just wrote start. It's okay because I've got thick skin, and God doesn't need me to defend him. Stay strong, brother.

A Devastating Loss

MY BROTHER, David, was now living in Pensacola, Florida, working as a painting contractor. I always enjoyed being with him, so I called to ask if he would be interested in coming home. The plan was to start our own painting business together. He agreed, and within a month, he was back home.

Both of us were good painters. I was more comfortable with repainting residential property, and he was more geared toward new construction. What started out as just two of us quickly expanded to nine employees. During our time together, we worked with 13 different building contractors.

David wasn't the best at dealing with new jobs and making bids or dealing with customer issues. I handled all of that, and he took charge of the job sites. This arrangement also made it possible for me to take another position with a plastics company as plant manager. The plant was about 45 minutes from where we lived. It was a good, well-paying job and proved my chops in business. I was successful with every job in my life. I was a major contrast to how I handled home life, which I hated.

On my way home from work every night, I picked up a six-pack of beer and a pint of vodka. I sat in the driveway and drank it before going into the house. My intention was to go in, eat, and go to bed, so I wouldn't have to speak to my wife. As I sat there one night, I looked up, and it hit me. We lived in a five-bedroom home with five bathrooms, three huge fireplaces, a glass-enclosed hot tub room, and a four-car garage in the best part of town. We both drove new vehicles. I had motorcycles and a toy hauler. Our kids had cars, and my oldest was a freshman in Bible college.

I said, "I did this. I freaking did this."

It wasn't her and all her so-called self-glorification. It was me. I was putting her through nursing school while I worked all the time. She made me believe all this time that I was nothing and couldn't make it without her. I walked into the house and packed enough clothes to carry on my bike. Ashley was enraged, screaming and hitting me.

My son walked in, and I said, "I love you, but I have to get out of here, son; I'll be back."

I never did go back. I spoke with my kids every day, but I never went home.

I filed for divorce and gave her everything except my motorcycle and personal property. She still ended up with my bike because she had my son testify that "I said I'd be back." The judge declared I abandoned my children and awarded her everything. I also had to pay sixteen hundred dollars a month for the kids. I can honestly say I never missed a payment. I didn't care. I was finally free from her after twenty-four years.

There's one thing I would like to add. If you remember my vows to my children when they were born, "to protect them?" Years after leaving, I found out I spent twenty-four years so my children wouldn't be hurt by another man, only to find out that my half-sisters were both molesting my two children and that their mother was physically and emotionally abusing them after I left. I tried; I swear I did. I never imagined the enemy would be within my own home.

Meth, God, and My Heart

My brother called and asked if we could meet. He told me that he had decided to go into the Army because he needed insurance for his family. I completely understood his reasoning. Even though we had a lot of work and made good money, we couldn't afford the cost of insurance for our employees. My brother made too much money to receive help from the state and not enough to pay for private insurance.

While my brother was getting things arranged to head off to boot camp, I started dating an office employee at the plant. We ended up living together and bought a townhome close to work. We laughed, had fun, and decided we would get married the following June.

While we were dating, we went to gentleman's clubs, danced, and drank continuously. I hadn't done any drugs in the first months of dating, and I told her, "Drugs are out of the question because they will destroy our relationship."

We started planning, and everything in my life seemed perfect for the first time. I really loved this woman.

One night at a club, an old friend of hers met us. We were dancing and having fun when I noticed they were leaving to go to the bathroom more frequently than normal. At closing time, she came to me and asked if we could go to her friend's house? I agreed, and we headed over there. We were there for about twenty minutes when out came the mirror, a straw, and cocaine. I now knew why the trips to the bathroom seemed odd.

Linda could use Friday and Saturday nights and then not think about it until the next weekend. I, on the other hand, could not. She and I were doing an eight ball on the weekend together, while I was doing three on my own, in secret, during the week. We began arguing more, the fun wasn't quite as fun, and money mysteriously came up missing. Addiction had once again taken hold of my soul.

We were a couple weeks from our wedding when I got a phone call from my dad. He said, "your mom needs you to come home."

It was midnight, so I said, "why, what is wrong?"

He repeated himself, "Your mom needs you to come home."

I said, "put mom on the phone."

Mom got on the phone and said, "Honey, I need you to come home." I started to ask why again, and then it hit me. My brother was in the war in Baghdad. I asked, and she confirmed; that my brother was dead. I screamed, fell to my knees, and just kept calling out his name.

We drove to my parents, and I remember screaming to God, "please, I'll be good. I'll do whatever you want, just please don't let him be gone!"

The next morning, the soldiers came to confirm that he was gone. My baby brother, my best friend, was dead. The funeral was beautiful, and he was honored by the city. I gave his eulogy, even though it was the hardest thing I'd ever done in my life.

My brother was supposed to come home for the wedding and be my best man. We put a picture of him in his place. We had a lot of family and guests unable to come because they were just in town for the funeral. Even though we were all saddened because of my brother's death, it was a beautiful wedding.

I was not ok. My brother was my best friend, and I loved him more than anyone on this earth. After he died, I started down an even darker place in my addiction. I wanted to die and started to try and kill myself with alcohol and drugs.

One night I had been asleep for a few hours when I woke up and sat on the side of the bed. I looked up, and my brother was standing there as clear as day. He said to me, "Are you ever going to sober up, so I can say goodbye to you?"

I screamed, "Never!"

He vanished as quickly as he appeared. I haven't seen him since.

Foster's Journal

They say they have a choice; they are just bums who want to get high, rather than get a job. They just want to blame everyone else for their problems.

The reality of it is that most addicts started using just like everyone else did. At a party, with friends, trying something for the first time, because it was bad, and they were being rebellious against their parents.

They didn't know that it would be different for them. That it would affect them in a way that someone never understood

They didn't know that our disease had been stirring inside of them their entire lives, the trouble, the lack of love they felt, The emptiness, the feeling doesn't feel like a big a load, and rejection felt by this world would now be eased by a substance or an addiction

They didn't know that they would soon lose sight and focus on what was important to them. Life itself for this person will never be the same. In the beginning, the addiction is fun and less frequent, and life seems to proceed as normal. Work, family, and friends are all stable. Social gatherings are welcome too, and finances haven't been affected. The world seems to be a better place, and life's problems seem to be nonexistent.

Eventually, without even realizing it's happening, the disease takes a stronger hold of the individual. What used to be a weekend habit is now three times a week plus the weekend. Missing work, avoiding family and friends wanting to be isolated is now a preference. Bills are now adding up, and finances are used on all the substances rather than everyday living expenses. Arguments with family members and friends become more frequent as they probed the attic with questions of concern. Everyone around the addict can see the changes happening, not even realizing quite a drastic event has occurred.

The addict will eventually break most connections with everyone they used to speak with regularly, leaving those individuals wondering what they've done wrong and with questions of why. The addict, now feeling guilty, will go into further isolation and regularly use in order to mask emotions of guilt and shame. Self-hatred or self-glorification becomes a new reflection in the mirror. Feeling the guilt of the damage they are causing in the lives of people they love begins a new journey of minimizing the situation. They start telling themselves they look okay or even better than before. The outside world sees them in a completely different way.

When the amount being used goes up, so does the price. Now the addict is having a hard time explaining where money is missing, why bills haven't been paid, and objects of value have disappeared. This brings more pressure from family, friends, and debt collectors. Most people are hesitant to believe the addict but go by the addict's past behavior and usually give in to the addict. The addict continues with the same pattern. This usually happens and bridges are burnt until the addict has no one to turn to. Until they find a new group to manipulate, con, and get sympathy from.

The addict is an award-winning actor, a hustler, a master manipulator, and the most cunning man ever invented. They will do anything to gain what they need to suppress all the emotions they don't want to face. Do they want to be this way, not usually? Would they stop if they knew how, more than likely? Do they truly love family and friends they now claim to hate; Yes? They just now have a disease that they don't know how to solve.

Rock bottom is usually the only way an addict starts to notice the need for a change. Overdose, loss of children, spouse, family, and friends can be a reason. Jail, prison, or violence are others. Death is the only other way out of addiction if a person hasn't hit rock bottom.

If a person could stop anytime they want, they are not an addict. They are a social person who uses to have fun, and they can make a choice anytime they want. A lot of society misunderstands that point. They think because they stopped when they wanted, everyone can do the same.

Looking for a Replacement

THE PLANT where my wife and I were working went bankrupt, so I started putting my resume out on the Internet. I was offered a position in the south for a major oil company managing an oil refinery. We moved and really loved where we ended up. Our home was right on the ocean, and it was beautiful. The area was a tourist attraction spot, so in the beginning, we spent a lot of time discovering new things and new places. We started to make friends, and on the outside, we seemed like the perfect couple.

We appeared happy, but inside I was miserable. I truly believe I died when my brother died. I was depressed and couldn't seem to come out of it. The drugs and the fact I was drinking a gallon of vodka every other day might of had something to do with it.

I worked a strange shift. It was three days on days, then four days off. I'd then work four days on the night shift and three days off. I hated it. I could never catch up on sleep. Days and nights were always messed up. Eventually, I secured another job on the day shift, managing a manufacturing plant.

When we first got together, we went out, partied, and had a lot of fun. After we married, her whole thought process changed. She wanted to stay home, and she spent all of her time on the couch with her face on the TV or on her computer. Our marriage had become stagnant and boring. We didn't communicate, so I once again engulfed myself in work and in drugs. I also started having an affair with an employee at my job. I was searching for someone or something to fill the void from the loss of my brother. Nothing worked.

There came a day when I hopped on my motorcycle for a ride. I came across some guys who belonged to one of the biggest motorcycle clubs in the world. We spoke, and they mentioned that I should come to the clubhouse and hang out with them. It wasn't long after that I was asked to be a prospect with the club. I loved being with the guys. Prospecting was a lot of work, but I didn't look at it that way. I enjoyed it. I went to work in the morning, then fulfilled my responsibilities as a prospect at night. I was gone all the time. At first, my wife would get upset, but after a while, she quit complaining. She went on a few rides with me but always seemed to think she was better than all of them. She stayed at home engrossed in her computer and TV while I was out to become one of the hardest bikers in our area.

It was a year and four months until I became a full-patched member. Everything changed once I was patched in. I now heard how the club made money and the dark side of the club a prospect wasn't able to know.

My wife now hated the club even more, and our relationship grew even farther apart. Methamphetamine became readily available, and I took advantage of it. My job was starting to be affected by my drug addiction, as well as my club life. The late-night parties that sometimes ran into the next day would cause me to miss work. It created even greater issues at home.

I tried to blame it all on my wife. I'd say, "If you wouldn't have changed, if you didn't sit on the couch all the time, we'd be ok!"

I'd also try to make her feel guilty for the cocaine that first night. A night that was six years ago by this time. It was all my fault, and I was losing the woman I loved because of my choices.

A new face appeared in the clubhouse one day. He was cocky, with a chip on his shoulder. He stood in the circle, and we asked him questions about why he wanted to join. There was nothing I liked about this guy. He had a year or more to change my mind.

One of the standard measures of a prospect how quickly he can respond to a brother who calls with a task. The prospects (unless at work) must drop whatever they're doing and answer that brother. The first prospect to carry out the task correctly gets praised by the brother, and he lets the other brothers know, which in turn gets you more praise. Those that didn't get there fast enough or didn't follow instructions got chastised by all.

I ordered a prospect to bring me an item that I needed yet would be difficult to find. Mr. Cocky, Jerry, arrived at my home within two hours, from across the city, with two, not just one, of what I needed. You might be thinking, "two hours?" That may seem like a long time, but you don't understand or know what I asked for. Plus, we lived in one of the biggest cities in the country.

We went into the backyard and sat there and talked for a couple hours. I found out he was a salesman for a concrete company. He was also responsible for taking customers on extravagant hunting trips all over the world and owned his own company that worked as contractors for the company he worked for. He impressed me, and I liked him. I wouldn't let him know that; not yet, anyway.

In the club, each prospect is given a sponsor, someone who spends time with the guy, showing him the ways of the MC world and proper protocol. Most people just think bikers wear colors, run around unorganized, acting crazy. The truth is, if you don't follow certain rules, you can get killed or start a war. How you introduce yourself, approach someone, and speak to them, are all done exactly the same way, or it causes disrespect. Examples: you never walk up into the middle of two patched brothers and interrupt them. You never put your hand out first when being introduced or wear a glove when preparing to shake a hand. You never turn your back on a brother, etc. You never let a brother walk alone or go to the restroom by themselves alone.

There's a proper way to say your name in an introduction, such as the name of the club, rank in that club, then riding name.

Jerry wasn't given to me to sponsor, but we started spending every day together because his sponsor worked odd hours. All prospects could be instructed, verbally disciplined, and called upon by any patched brother. To be able to physically discipline, the sponsor had to agree and vote upon. Prospects were also not allowed to be involved in criminal acts.

One day we were in the downtown area of the city at a car auction he was involved in. We were on our way back to his house, which was forty-five minutes away, when he hit a huge pothole in the road. It bent his front wheel, and he could ride only twenty miles per hour at the most. He looked at me and said, "you can go ahead; I'll make it home."

"First of all, I would never leave you. Secondly, you don't tell me what I'll do, prospect."

The only way we were going to make it home was to go through one of the worst wards in the city. The people who lived in these wards were known to kill police officers for coming into the ward. White people, unless raised there, were definitely not welcome in the area. They knew better and avoided it always. Usually, anyone that ended up there unintentionally was a tourist that immediately regretted the wrong turn.

We stopped at a gas station right before the entrance to the highway. I had him take a hammer and a piece of cardboard to try and straighten the rim. Once he was done, I looked at him and said, "You ready?"

"For...what," he asked.

I looked ahead at the entrance, and he looked at me, and chuckled. "No way, are you serious?"

"Can your bike go sixty down the freeway? Then I'm dead serious," I said.

We started our bikes and headed towards the entrance. I had my colors on, and he had his prospect patch on. Immediately, a car came in behind us. Black people were hollering at us from the housing projects. The car would get close but never came at us aggressively. They knew better. There may have only been two of us, but they respected my colors. They also knew I could make a call and have thousands of brothers there quickly.

We rode through that entire ward without incident. From that day on, he and I were tighter than any brother I had in the club. The more time he and I spent together, the more we obviously learned about each other.

He had a wife, a daughter, and a beautiful home. His "man cave" was bigger than most people's homes. He bought and had a company restore vehicles, so he could resell them. Yes, he had a perfect life; or so it appeared.

I was off work one day, trying to score dope when we ran into each other. I was on my bike as always, and so was he. I said, "what are you doing on this side of town?"

He looked at me like he didn't want to tell me. I said, "Whenever you're in that cut, your business is my business. What are you doing?"

"Making a pick-up," he said.

"You do dope; since when?" I asked.

I knew he didn't do drugs. An addict can spot an addict anywhere. Plus, we'd spent so much time together I'd know if he was. "No, it's for someone else. I just do the pick-up and take it to them."

This piqued my interest because this means, if it wasn't club-sanctioned, he was working for someone that was cutting into our profits. "What are you picking up? Who are you working for?" I asked.

Come to find out, he was picking up for a couple. He found a girlfriend online. He moved her, and her husband from out West to our city. He rented them an apartment and bought them their heroin. He would then sleep with this girl, while the husband was in the other room. The husband knew it. The wife did it. All for their dope. I eventually went to check on them with him, and she was dead. Husband was close to it, but we left him anyway.

This guy, my brother was a piece of dirt. He just got away with it because he had money. He slept with his sister-in-law. Even helped her start a small shop, so he could sleep with her on certain days. Come to find out though, all the money was his wife's.

I thought I had found a friend who could replace the whole left in my life when my brother died. We had some great times together, but he turned out to be a bigger looser than me. I was starting to feel desperate. Perhaps there was no way for me to build a life that amounted to anything. Perhaps I was destined do die in a drug induced stupor, lying in an alley, with no friends or family in my life.

I wanted to be more than a statistic, another drug causality.

Foster's Journal

I'm an addict. I'm an addict...

I will lie, steal, manipulate, and become whoever I need to...

So I could fulfill my deed, hide my emotional scars, not going to feel like you do.

I hate who I am, and what I've done...

My fixe is my love as they say trust no one.

To love me is to be hurt by me, you see...

I will turn out all my friends and family.

I'm sorry you worried about me, feel pain, and I make you cry...

Sleepless nights, searching for me, I know you tried.

Let go of the hurt, the paid, and the anger you feel...

Try to think of the person who watched you, the one that was most real.

I promise I love you all more than I could say,

I wish I could take back playing with addiction that first day.

I didn't know it would happen, it's not your fault but your mind at ease... I'm an addict just like cancer, I have a disease.

If you're reading this don't be sad, try not to cry...

I'm an addict, my freedom comes when I die.

Putting Life Back Together

After the incident with the club, I contacted my daughter, Rachel. She and her family were living up north, and I asked if I could stay with her for a while. She immediately agreed, drove to where I was, and picked me up. When she arrived in town, she was exhausted and needed to rest. I didn't have a home, so I asked around some of the people I knew. There weren't that many to choose from since I had just lost the majority of the people I knew. I took my daughter and granddaughter to the safest place I knew. A place that I knew she would hate, but a place I knew she could rest, and there was no threat of anyone messing with her or the baby, so I made the call.

When we arrived at the gate, my daughter looked at me and said, "what is this place, Dad?"

I told her the truth just like I always had all her life. I never hid my lifestyle from my children. I never had drugs in my home, nor did they ever see me use drugs. They, unfortunately, saw me under the influence far too many times and felt the heartbreak of being the child of a drug addict. They used to tell their friends when they became teenagers, "drugs are bad, just ask my dad." They would laugh about it, but it cut me to the core.

I said, "Rachel, this is a compound for a group of people who hate other colors and nationalities."

Her jaw dropped, and she replied, "you're a skinhead!"

I assured her I was not. They were just people I had contact with and nothing more. As I finished that statement, the gate started to open. It was one of those big steel, electric gates that looked like it should be on the front of a prison, not a home. We were met by two men with rifles and shaved heads. They both walked up and gave me a hug, and said hello to my daughter. They walked us up to the house but then turned and went back to the place where they met us.

As we entered, my friend DJ met us with a big smile on his face and arms wide open. Dave was a short man with swastika tattoos everywhere. He had a black eye patch covering his left eye. It had been injured in a prison fight, and he lost his vision in it. He was short, built like a bulldog, and handsome but could make someone move to the other side of the street just by his appearance. DJ was like so many others I've known; if they love you, they'll die for you. If they don't, they will kill you in a heartbeat.

"Brother" where the hell have you been?"

I explained all the issues I'd had with the club, Jerry, and to watch out for the snake.

He said, "Let's take care of business, and I got your back, brother," but I assured him there was nothing to worry about.

The look on my daughter's face was priceless. You could tell she liked the attention and respect I was receiving but wanted nothing to do with these people. So, what did DJ do? Walked right up, gave my daughter a big hug, and said, "Welcome, whatever you need, I got, and whatever I don't have, I'll get. Just say the word."

"I need a shower and some sleep," Rachel said. DJ whistled and told some tweaked-out woman to take care of Rachel.

Rachel finished her shower, came out of the bathroom, and teased, "Dad!" I was in the back room finishing up getting high with DJ ."

I came out, and Rachel was standing there. She said, "Dad I feel better now, can we just go ahead and go?"

I agreed, we said our goodbyes, and we left.

We were down the road for maybe five hours, and I could tell Rachel was exhausted. She had driven thirteen hours to pick me up, showered, and started all over again. I suggested getting a hotel room so she could rest, and she gave in. Before we made it to the hotel room, Rachel said, "Oh man, now what?"

I looked in the side mirror and saw red and blue lights flashing behind us. Rachel pulled over, and the officer came up to her window and stated that her plates were expired. Rachel had the new registration in the car; her husband had forgotten to put them on. The officer asked for both of our driver's licenses. He walked back to his car and fed our information into the system. He got out of his car and walked toward my side of the car. He asked me to step out of the vehicle and walk in between the two cars.

I wasn't surprised by this; it comes with the lifestyle I chose to live; I was also flagged in the system as a "known member of my ex-club," and I am on the FBI watch list. The officer asked me multiple questions like, "who was the woman with me?" "Do I have any weapons?"

He said, "there have been women getting kidnapped and used in sex trafficking rings." I assured him that Rachel was my daughter and that I knew nothing of a trafficking ring. He then proceeded to ask Rachel the exact same questions and then let us go. All of that was familiar territory, and I didn't sweat it at all, even with the eight ball of meth in my pocket that DJ had given me as a going-away present.

We arrived at Rachel's home the next evening after spending the night in the hotel. It was great to see my daughter and grandkids. Their home was beautiful, and it was in a great location. It didn't take long before I started to feel like an intruder, lonely and out of place.

Rachel's husband worked a lot and was rarely home. I started to miss my friends and my life back home, but I didn't have anywhere to go back to, so I went into a dark depression. I spent most of my time feeling sorry for myself and thinking of ways I could escape reality. The eight ball I had didn't last long, and I had to come down without Rachel and her husband knowing.

The thing about methamphetamine is you get seriously angry during withdrawal. It brings up extreme emotions that are usually covered up with the drug. Rachel's husband was offered a transfer to another state with his company. He accepted it, and we moved cross country. My son lived there, so I was excited to see him, and it was someplace I'd never been. It didn't take long for all the depression to come flooding back in, so I left.

I decided to go back home where my parents lived. I knew I wouldn't be able to stay with them because of my lifestyle and some past issues, but at least I'd be closer to them, and I'd be able to see them whenever I could. I wasn't sure where I would stay, but I just wanted to be home with family and familiar surroundings.

I ran into an old employee one day after I got back, and he offered me a place to stay at his house. He was a single man, and we shot compound bow tournaments together as a team, so I accepted. I was looking forward to moving in, as he said it was an upper apartment and that I could have all of the space to myself. It seemed like my future was looking brighter; until I walked in, that is. I have been in drug dens and shooting galleries that were better than this place.

I have never seen such a dirty, disgusting place in my life. The dishes were piled up, and dirty. There were piles of dog poop all over the floor and trash everywhere. The upstairs was the cleanest part of the entire house, and it was filthy. It took me hours to clean it up enough to feel comfortable to even sit down. There was no AC, and only a mattress on the floor, so it was extremely hot and uncomfortable. I, however, was exhausted and ready to sleep.

I fell asleep and woke up the next morning dripping in sweat; I was also covered with small bite marks from the top of my head to the soles of my feet. You guessed it, bed bugs. I was completely angry, emotionally drained, and suicidal. I was just fed up with life going negatively.

I was in my fifth day of living in this swill of a home when my mom contacted me, letting me know my dad was scheduled for a heart procedure the next day. She asked me if I would like to sit with her while he was in the procedure and spend the night with her that night, as he had to stay overnight? I happily agreed as she told me they'd pick me up the next morning.

"Mom, I feel like Pharoah," I said. "I've lost everything. My kids, my people (meaning the club), and now I have bugs and sores all over me."

My Mom, who always told me the blunt truth said, " Maybe God's trying to tell you something, son? Don't you think it's time you get back to where you belong?"

I, as always, knew she was right but brushed it off.

My Dad came out of the procedure with no complications and had to stay in the hospital for a few days. As Mom and I were talking about God and my life, next to my dad's bedside, he said, "do you want to come home, son? Do you want to come to stay with your mom and me?"

I have to admit, Mom and I looked at each other and smiled, thinking Dad was under the influence of some sort of narcotic, and his statement was because of that. He opened his eyes and said, "Do you want to come to stay with us? If you do, you realize there are rules you must live by?"

"Yes, Dad, I want to come home. Thank you," I said.

I knew exactly what Dad meant when he said "rules." It meant I had a curfew, he was in control, and whenever they were in church, so was I. I honestly hated the thought of it but knew I needed to be somewhere safe, and I needed to be nurtured. So, Mom and I took all my stuff, washed it at a commercial laundry mat, and I went home.

Foster's Journal

Addiction isn't a choice or a lifestyle that people enjoy. It affects everyone in their life. It costs them everything and eventually kills them if they don't find help.

Addicts need people who see addiction just as they would see heart disease or a stroke. The doctors involved in doing research need to learn from addicts who have been through addiction and not lab rats. Scientific research is an important part of helping this disease, but the heart and reality of it all are that it doesn't diagnose the internal turmoil the addict feels.

Addiction doesn't have to be a part of the world we live in, or it can be greatly reduced if addiction is treated as it should be.

Addiction is a lack of love. Somewhere, somehow, and sometimes, a person came to believe they weren't loved, and they found a substance, or an action, goodies that are a missing part of their lives.

A Broken Heart – Physically and Emotionally

BEING AT home was an adjustment. I had always been the black sheep of the family, you know, the drug addict. They never wanted to get to know me or find out why. It was easier to label me and put me over to the side. Even with my mom, there were several years when I stayed away from her, didn't talk to her, or had anything to do with her.

Things changed. Since she and my stepdad got together, she changed. She was now a Christian, and every time I tried to talk with her about my abuse and other experiences, she always said, "That's under Jesus' blood," meaning everything had been forgiven. When she would tell me that, I would think of my four children that never got to be a part of her life, and I wanted to snatch the life right out of her. I couldn't understand how someone could allow a child to be hurt. I had promised to take care of mine from the minute of their birth.

But we made it through, my mom and me. She was not a Christian at the time. Without a relationship with God, she didn't know any better. It's easy to complain about how bad your parents are until you become a parent and realize it's not that easy. I don't think Mom had anything to do with the Satanic rituals, but I know that if she did and tried to stop it, Steve would have put her in the ground. He hit her often, and she was afraid of him. Although my grandparents were good people, I don't think they taught her how to be a good mother and build a family.

My sister and I have discussed it, trying to figure out why Mom went wrong. I think it was just my dad, my real dad. He was nothing more than a piece of scum. Remember, he was Mom's second husband. Her first was a decent man. He even offered to adopt me when she got pregnant, willing to provide for me even though Mom was with someone else. She wouldn't do it. For some reason, she just couldn't keep her pants on. I'm realistic about my mom. She did a lot of stupid stuff.

All of us are who we are because of circumstances. And you know what? There's nothing in my life that I would change. I say that honestly because I help people. I can help people with so many different issues. You know, I talk to addicts every day, and that's the key to success. This is how I can use this? How God can be a difference for somebody else. I share my story with anybody who will listen. I'm on the addiction websites every day, and I get tons and tons of responses.

And I'm 51 years old now, yet I still have to lock the bathroom door before using the facilities. I must keep the front door locked and windows covered just to feel safe. It takes everything I have just to get past my past. The struggle with all the consequences of my life's experiences will always be with me. They are not going away, but I can cope with God's presence and help. I have a purpose for as long as God leaves me here.

I spoke earlier of my initial experience with God when He spoke to me through a vision. That experience stuck with me;

I've known since then that being in front of large groups of people would happen.

My stepfather, Ernie, ran an alcohol and drug recovery program. He wanted me to take it over when I settled back at home. However, I couldn't. I was still an active addict, but he didn't know that. I kept it a secret from everyone. You've heard of "functioning alcoholics," people who go to work and perform like everyone else while being an alcoholic. I was a functioning junkie. I took the drugs to cope, not to alter my behavior. They were such an important part of my physical system that people didn't know I was using.

Mom and my stepfather were involved with a Christian ministry called Harvester's Fellowship that provided opportunities for speaking and ministry. Because no one knew I continued to use drugs, I was invited to speak to a church youth group. It went well and took off from there. The invitations came frequently from churches all over Tennessee, Kentucky, and Indiana. They even provided my ordination. Soon I found myself speaking nearly every week, sometimes multiple times. Speaking about my life created numerous triggers, so I sought therapy.

People all over the Midwest invited me to come and share my story. It told of my childhood, early drug use, and molestation. I included the story about the vision I had at camp and how it was now coming true. Each service ended with an altar call, just like the one I responded to at camp.

I constantly felt hypocritical. I was talking about God's goodness and salvation, yet I was still addicted. I don't know how to make it sound any better. In my guilt, I always prayed that God would use me. I always had numerous people coming to the altar, so obviously, it wasn't me. God was doing something. Still, I felt guilty, dirty. I wasn't doing it for financial gain because I wasn't making any money. I did it because I wanted to share.

The last time I spoke was in Indiana. A friend of mine, one of my closest friends, attends the church. He's like my closest brother, and I was higher than a kite on methamphetamine. Numerous people came down to the altar, but when I got done, I said I'll never do this again, and I didn't preach a day after that.

My friend never knew. Nobody knew. I did drugs for so long and for so many years that it was just a morning routine. I got up. I shot up. I went on with my day and went to work. I also needed it to sleep every night. It was just like taking my heart medication.

In September of 2020, I began feeling run down, like I was drowning and couldn't catch a breath. Fluids were also building up, causing my body to be swollen. I finally went to the emergency room. After running a series of tests, they diagnosed me with congestive heart failure. The left side of my heart is quickly dying. It really got my attention when they told me I essentially had the heart of an 83-year-old man.

The first step was to install a pacemaker and defibrillator in my chest to regulate my heart. The only cure to fix the problem is a heart transplant, and my history of drug use prevents me from getting on the list for a donor's heart.

After getting back on my feet, I began speaking once again. While at a Speaker Jam in Arizona, I passed out in the hotel lobby and was rushed to the hospital. The pacemaker and defibrillator had become septic, and sepsis was running rampant throughout my body. Consequently, the pacemaker and defibrillator had to be removed and could not be replaced. My stay in the hospital lasted a month, and I had as many as eight strokes in one day while there. One was massive and paralyzed my entire left side. Fortunately, it all came back. I went from taking no medicine to 30 pills every day.

But my heart has not improved. Basically, I'm waiting to die, and it could happen any day. It's the price of more than 40 years of drug use.

Currently, I have a very good relationship with my daughter. Not so much with my son. When my kids were little, I told them, no matter what, respect your mother and honor your mother, protect your mother, even though I couldn't stand her, I hate that my son took that to heart, and he chose his mother. I haven't talked to him in eight years. Which is hard since I'm dying.

It took a long time, but my use of drugs taught me some valuable lessons. The most obvious is that there is always a better way. I don't make excuses, but I do understand how it happened. My life was filled with people who used and abused me. But I couldn't quit. Ten minutes after I got home from the long stay in the hospital in Arizona, I was in the garage shooting up methamphetamine. My heart was working at 17% capacity, and it was not enough to get me to quit.

I was sitting at the house with little ability to do anything, and I began searching social media for addiction groups. I quickly discovered loads of people with addiction problems. After a short time, I just said, "Screw it," and started writing my story.

As I posted stuff to the groups, the response was overwhelming. People were hungry to find someone who understood. The only thing I had to offer was transparency. I didn't care what they thought of me; sometimes, I was harsh. It was for me to get some kind of healing from all the crap I was carrying. I realized that I was trying to heal myself.

Suddenly, people started responding to what I was writing, saying, "Foster, I need you to help me. Can you help me?"

I didn't lie. I told them I was still active in addiction. I didn't try to cover up anything. I didn't tell them they could get cured.

Ultimately, I received a text from a mother who asked for help because her babies were in active addiction, and I was the only one she thought could help them. Right then, I made a choice to quit being a hypocrite. It was important to be honest with the people in the online group. I didn't care about myself. I cared about the other people.

I love helping people when they're hurting and in the middle of stuff because I know what it's like to be there, so I stopped. I began writing more and helping more and more people. I don't know what it is other than God. That's all I can say because I'm a worthless piece of crap. But God uses me to help people, and that's how I got clean. It was because I cared more about others, to be honest.

My parents have both died. My stepfather's issues that caused them to invite me back to their home, eventually caught up with him. Mom died of Covid on November 4, 2021. They were beautiful people. I espcially miss my mother and have always regretted that we missed so much of life together. I look forward to a soon reunion with her in eternity.

Thoughts on Addiction

Addiction isn't a choice or a lifestyle that people enjoy. It affects everyone in their life. It costs them everything and eventually kills them if they don't find help.

Addicts need people who see addiction just like heart disease or a stroke. The doctors involved in research need to learn from addicts who have been through addiction, not lab rats. Scientific research is an important part of helping this disease, but the heart of it and the reality is that it doesn't diagnose the internal turmoil or pain the addict feels.

Addiction doesn't have to be a part of our world, or it can be greatly reduced if treated as it should be.

Addiction is a lack of love. Somewhere, somehow, a person came to believe they weren't loved, and they found a substance or an action that was a missing part of their lives.

This will infuriate and possibly cause a lot of disruption. It is not my intention. My intention is to speak the truth in love, but the truth.

I am Jehovah, and there is none else; besides me there is no God. (Isaiah 45:5 American Standard Bible)

For many months I have been struggling with the higher power and a God of your understanding. Not trying to figure it out, but the fact that we don't share the truth about him.

In the 1930s, when AA began, it was solely based on godly principles. It was changed because people weren't coming to AA because they were not believers. I truly believe in the step work of AA, and I believe that our predecessors knew exactly what they were doing when they began these programs. However, I question the fact that we don't speak the truth about God.

Do we say anything can be your higher power or God of your own understanding to make people feel comfortable or hope they will somehow find their way to the one true God? There is an order to the spiritual realm of things."

Believe in God that he sent his son to die on the cross for our sins.

Repent and confess our sins. Repentance means to turn from and not do it again.

There's nothing in the Bible about a Salvation prayer.

It's not about a church building but a relationship with God.

It's about speaking with him, listening to him, and asking for His will in my life.

Most of us had an issue with God because we were hurt by someone, were told He wasn't real or had been hurt by a human in the name of God. Not God. God is a gentleman. He doesn't force himself on us. He's a quiet voice that says I love you; I want to be in your life. That's who God is.

In the second paragraph, the first sentence of the NA literature, "Why are we here?" It says, "Most of us realized that we were slowly committing suicide in our addiction, but addiction is such a cunning enemy of life that we had lost the power to do anything about it.

That sentence hits me deep inside my inner core; it is one of many that brings me to the realization that my life is not my own. I've been in and out of the rooms for 30 plus years and read the above statement thousands of times. Not once have I read it "clean," yet everyone around me believed me to be.

I can look a person in the face and tell them the truth about my entire life without hesitation. I lay out all the sexual abuse, Satanic rituals, and verbal and physical abuse out there in hopes it'll help someone, but I cannot say please help me, I'm dying here, and I don't know how to stop! So I could tell you to slowly commit suicide each and every day.

My silence is my shame, and my isolation is my guilt. The reminder that I have failed every individual I've come in contact with in this group, given advice to, and led to believe that I was doing well when I, in fact, was not. No... I am not in self-pity, and no... I don't believe my life is worse than yours. It's not a competition... We all lose if we're keeping score.

My "disease" is not cunning and baffling." It's my life, my reality, and has been since I was five. It doesn't trick me each day. I wake up and make a choice to stick, check, and push.

I know God hasn't gone anywhere and that He's real. There is no doubt in my mind. I just can't find the courage to trust him.

I also know that those of you who love me really love me. I also thank you for it. Those of you who don't know me or never read my writing will think I'm stupid, and that's okay. I write for me, not you.

The reason for this conversation is to say I've earned my seat at an NA meeting. I have a desire to stop using, but I know the reality is that I never will. I don't know anything different. Sadly I know there is an order to things, and I will end up in hell.

I love you all. I hope you know that. I haven't been on Facebook in months, and I won't be for a long time, if ever. I just thought of all of you who've given time from your lives to be should know.

★★★★★★★★★★★★★★★★★★★★★★★★★★★

I've been through so many things in my life, just as the majority of people in this group have. It made me a fighter and definitely able to take a punch. It also made me afraid of very little. I've worked through most of my childhood trauma for the most part. The forced drug use, the physical, emotional, and verbal abuse are not who I am but a part of what makes me who I am.

I could share my story with anyone who asks and work with people who want help and advice without having any triggers.

When I sleep through the night, my mind is tormented with nightmares, cold sweats, and physical feelings that take over. I hate the dark and wake up many nights with what seems to be hovering over me cloaked, making me feel suffocated. It just moves back and forth as if it's waiting to attack. I sometimes see figures moving back and forth in my room and hear whispers. I'm writing this while I'm clean, and these things happen when I'm clean. Stop talking, shadow people.

It makes me wonder if subconsciously I haven't really dealt with things in my past or if I'm just under attack from the enemy. My sexual abusers always came at night when I was a child. I'd wake up, and he'd be standing over me in a drunken vodka stupor and hurt me.

I have never slept well since I was a child. Three or four hours is usually the most sleep I get at night. With my heart issue, it's sometimes even less than that. Maybe I pushed all the crap so deep that I just don't feel it anymore, and it still needs to be dealt with?

Maybe I get bored because there are no drugs in my system to cover up the crap inside my heart, head, and soul. Real recovery is hard because it's not just about stopping drug use. It's about heading all of you in the same direction. LOL! It's very freaky exhausting.

★★★★★★★★★★★★★★★★★★★★★★★★★★★

Meth, God, and My Heart

I had so many responses to my last post that it amazed me. Words of encouragement, concern, and sympathy. It took me a bit to respond to such kindness.

I would like to say something, so everyone knows how I feel about the trauma I endured as a child. The story I told you was actually mild in comparison to others. Still, I wanted to be conscious of others who may have received similar trouble in their lives. Triggers are extremely real.

I forgive each and every person that has ever beaten, molested me, or given me drugs at such an early age. I hold no anger, nor is it in my heart to harm any of them. It happened. It's real, and it tore me up. It also made me who I am today as a man, with a few extra twists and turns of my own. You're all screaming how!

I spent a long time hating them, plotting their deaths or how I would get my revenge. I actually did with one of them, and it changed me forever.

I realized that all the time I spent thinking and feeling hate for them was only hurting me. It was destroying me, actually. They were still controlling me inside my mind, and I was letting them. I guarantee you most of them never even think of me anymore. Why? Because it's more than likely, that they had multiple victims after me. Not that it makes it any better. It actually makes it much worse.

If I hate them, then both of us need help. Would I be of any asset to someone if I said to hate them? No, it would only destroy both of us. Hating only breeds more hate, bitterness, or resentment, and the cycle will always continue.

Let me make something perfectly clear. Forgiveness does not mean I forget. I'll never forget what happened to me, never. The truth of the matter is that I want to be able to relate to the addict who has been sexually traumatized. Not that it's fun to walk down that road all the time. To me, it's worth it. In my eyes and heart, I know that God loves you. I was strong enough to handle, break the cycle, and help others with it.

I would not change one second of my life if it means someone is able to be restored from their own abuse and experience. I'm not trying to minimize all your comments, and since your feelings about my childhood situation. I just want to let you know that I'm at peace with everything.

★★★★★★★★★★★★★★★★★★★★★★★★★★★

The hardest part about being an addict in recovery is the constant ups and downs. One day you're on top of the world, and everything seems perfect. Life could not be better. The next day you feel as if you get the depths of hell and hate the entire world. Life could not get any worse.

The life of an addict in recovery is like riding the most extreme roller coaster ever. If you happen to be close to that individual, standing and staring right next to them, and feeling every twist, turn, highs, lows, and hoopty do's in their life. I can't imagine having to deal with someone like me.

The truth is most people in an addict's life can't handle it. They don't know how; it's too scary. It's overwhelming, and it makes them sick. They usually jump off the ride before it's even close to being over. Guess what. They should not have accepted it, been okay with it, or even wanted it. It's absolutely contrary to the lives most of them live. They also end up brokenhearted, feeling rejected and guilty. They don't know why because they did all they could get, they feel as if the addict's life is somehow their fault.

In recovery, I've learned that I must make it my business to watch out for other's emotions and feelings. Although I'm clean, I'm still capable of being that old self-centered person who takes without giving, is loved but doesn't love, and controls without having self-control.

It's a self-preservation tactic. A tactic I learned as a child. Recovery is selfish and takes a lot of hard work. That selfishness should stop right there, and we become someone who gives back what was given to us. People genuinely loved us. We just have to learn to see what they see and generally love ourselves. The weak need to be loved back.

I had a talk with someone tonight who was very real; whether or not you believe in such things, it's up to you. I was here, had the conversation, and I'm not here to impress you. Read on or scroll by; the choice is yours.

I've never in my entire life slept well at night. Nightmares have always been a reality for me. Tonight is no different. I woke up and headed to the garage to grab a cig. But I was finished. I started back upstairs and heard, "I haven't left you."

I spun with my elbow going into cracked-up mode. There's no one here. Have you ever been embarrassed that no one else was even around? That was me, and I laughed it off.

I have a split-level home on an acreage. It's me, my dog, and a ton of waterfowl on the pond, so I pay attention when I hear someone's voice. As I come up to the top landing, I hear, "I've known you since you were a little boy. I've always made sure you were taken care of. You've never needed anything because of me. I put the right people in front of you to give you success and comfort."

I could feel this person breathing on my neck. I could feel each word spoken, making my skin crawl. He said you can't see me because I don't want you to see me. You've seen me before, though. You've spoken with me. We've laughed, cried, had bad times and good times. I was there for the first time, and the last time I was there when Daddy put the needle in your arm at 14. I was there with you when you were 28 and had your first heart attack. I was there when you got home from the hospital, remember that day? They said you were dying and pulling for Red ten minutes later in the garage. I even invited friends to join me. They all remember you too. After all those years, I stood beside you. All the times I comforted you, gave you courage when you were afraid. Gave you strength when you were weak and eager to do things. I helped you ride to the top and so many ways. But you no, you ungrateful piece of s***, I think it's okay to kick me to the curb. Tell me you don't need me, they are going a different way. Who do you think you are?"

I could feel the anger radiating from this voice. They were gritting their teeth so hard it made mine hurt. It screamed, "You will come back to me! You will want to search for me just as you have always, and always will! I was beside you from day one and will finish my task."

I said, what the hell is going on? Am I losing my mind? I turned around and said, "Who are you, and what do you want?"

Its voice was deep and evil, then it said quickly, "What I've always wanted... You. My name is addiction. Do you remember me now? I'll see you soon..."

Epilogue

ALL MY life up until I got clean from IV drug use, I wondered, "why me?" "Why did I have to be molested, be used in satanic rituals, given drugs at the age of five, shot up with meth at fourteen by my dad?" "Why did I have to be tortured, beaten, and go to thirteen different schools before seventh grade because we were running from my mom's five husbands or boyfriends?"

What did I do to deserve any of it? Then I think of my Savior being beaten, spit upon, mocked, and crucified, being speared to finish His life. He didn't deserve any of it either, but he bore it all for me and every other person in the world.

I then think of the scripture: You intended to harm me, but God intended it for good to accomplish what is now being done, the saving of many lives. (Genesis 50:20)

By no means am I comparing myself to Jesus. I just know that the devil tried to kill me from birth and didn't succeed, and God took all those things that happened to me, using them for His glory.

I can talk with an addict. I can speak with those traumatized by sexual, physical, and emotional abuse. I can sympathize with the person begging for money and food, not knowing where they will sleep or how they'll stay warm on those cold nights.

I don't ask "why me" anymore. I say thank you, God, that it was me, for giving me another day to use it for your glory.

In His Grip,
Foster

www.ingramcontent.com/pod-product-compliance
Lightning Source LLC
LaVergne TN
LVHW052256070426
835507LV00035B/3045